The  m

Unadulterated Truths to Consider About the

Path to Parenthood

Ashton Saldana

For Jaidyn Leon & Luca Dash—
You are the closest I will ever have to my own
children, and you are all I will ever need.

Table of Contents

Introduction

I felt a deep pull to write this tiny book to spread awareness about a subject that hits close to home for me. These are merely my feelings and thoughts, not to disabuse your lifestyles and opinions that differ from mine. Simply, I want my readers to own the choice to live the life they desire and not feel alone if they choose not to have children. The Parenthood Pendulum will serve as a manual for the millennial woman to help her navigate through life choices and follow a path that will lead to her most fulfilled life. The woman of today is now presented with the option to choose alternative lifestyles and is no longer expected to conform to the traditional way of life; marriage, children, and running a household. With this societal shift, I believe women today are in need of empowerment, support, and confidence to decide what choices are best for them. Many find themselves imitating the lives of females that surround them even though they may be more enthused, inspired, and stimulated by a different vision.

I have personally endured the pressure to conform to societal norms and now I am using my experience to encourage others to be in charge of their one life to live. We are seeing a shift in women prioritizing career goals, marrying later in life, and having serious conversations with their partner regarding if having children is even on their trajectory. This dialogue is monumental and a clear evolution of society. Even 20 years ago, a strong woman in the workplace or childless by choice was an unusual path for a female. Although, I think there is still a stigma associated with women who decide to make unconventional life choices and we need to diminish that and allow all trails to be widely accepted nor questioned.

I have staunchly decided that children are not a part of my life path, but I too was once unsure and at a crossroads with what I truly wanted. My book will discuss the many women I have encountered who deeply desired to have children, but circumstances didn't allow, and they have managed to achieve joy and find purpose in their life. When faced with this intended or unintended pivot, it's imperative that people feel supported in redirecting the course of their lives while dealing with insensitive commentary and intrusive questions.

Some feel matrimony is a means to starting a family, while others value the commitment made to one another but do not intend on expanding their family unit. Some have created beautiful family dynamics without making it legally binding. We do not live in a one-size-fits-all society and I encourage the reader to ask themselves questions, embark on soul-searching opportunities, and discover their purpose and passions that will aid them in making the right decisions for the one person that truly matters: themselves.

Not only is this relatable content to the childless population but this book is intended to eradicate misconceptions placed by society. I hope to aid in bridging the gap between those who want

& have children and those with opposing perspectives. Throughout the book, you will read quotes from the numerous women and men that I had the privilege to confabulate with and they fearlessly shared it all. I know you will find their stories wildly different and yet, equally inspiring. I am forever grateful to the contributors for using their voice to help reform the narrative of what it is to be childfree and what parenting really entails.

Chapter 1
My Journey to a Childfree Life

I identify myself as an "early-articulator" when it comes to my decision not to have children. Early on, I knew I wasn't put on this earth to be a mother. My earliest memory of not wanting to be a mom was when I was 12 years old. Yes, I had baby dolls growing up, but my imaginary life consisted of me dropping the baby off at daycare because I was a doctor and had to get to work. My friend Stacey who is also childless by choice stated "I definitely wasn't the one to push a stroller around! The one doll I had I ripped their leg off." She continued by saying, "the maternal instinct just never showed up for me and I'm really grateful for that." When I would vocalize this presentiment, I was assured by most older female figures that I would "change my mind." This left me confused because I was content with my mind not changing. I didn't feel that having children would define me or make me a better woman, but I quickly realized that society felt differently. Regardless of the unsolicited opinions and judgments from my immediate family and the external world, I kept true to knowing what I felt and didn't waiver on that. I am proud of my bravery in not worrying about meeting certain expectations or comparing my life to others. I love the skin I'm in. I own my choices, sexuality, and authenticity. I am not lonely, defective, or a failure.

Our entire lives we've been confronted with the narrative that a female is worthy once she a) gets married, and b) has children. As we slowly progress, the idea of a woman who chooses not to marry and/or bear children is more prominent. We have more women openly talking about their decision to focus on running for office rather than running a household. We see many successful, happy, and fulfilled women who happen to be single or have decided not to have children. Even though the "spinster," "cat lady," and "old maid" labels have decreased, let's be real, the stigma is still alive and well.

Motherhood was never particularly fascinating to me. I never had what one would call a "motherly instinct." I am greatly aware of my limitations and moreover, I felt my life was destined for something beyond motherhood. I married at age 23. I expressed to my then-husband my position on children and that I truly didn't feel that marriage was synonymous with motherhood. He accepted my position, assuming I would change my mind, while I was confident he would acquire my same beliefs. After six years of marriage and 30 fast approaching, this conversation seemed to rear its ugly head more often than not. The pressure from family and my lack of confidence to stand my ground got me to entertain the idea of motherhood. Feeling inescapable, I took the first step and stopped taking my birth control. I wasn't remotely excited about the idea and I was more concerned with the resentment I'd have towards this child. Needless to say, I was back on birth control seven months later. He wanted a family more than anything and I had to respect that, yet I realized that living anything other than a childfree life was non-negotiable for me. I didn't want to be filled with frustration for being forced to bring life into this world, knowing that it wasn't something I wanted nor was suited for. The dissolution of my marriage began and we both had the courage to walk away from a union that was no longer serving us. I knew happiness could be found outside the bounds of a conventional marriage and becoming a mother so I was eager to pursue that.

Moving forward, it was crucial I held onto my truths and broached the subject early on with prospective partners. I made a vow to the most important person in my life - myself. The vow was to never do anything I didn't want to do, never let go of my belief in the person I am, I want to be, and the person I will be, but moreover to never fall back into a lackluster life where I am living for others. There were years of falling victim to societal pressures of living a "normal" life, but finally, I can say that I am living as the person I've always wanted to be.

I accepted my unconventional life choices, including my choice not to have children, despite the fact that other people hadn't. I invite you to challenge society's rules and live unapologetically. There have been generations of women that have preceded me but conformed instead of living out their authentic self. I want to pave a path for my niece, your daughters, and sisters to not stay in relationships, careers, or lifestyles because they are worried, afraid, or unaware that they have a choice. Many of our mothers and grandmothers took up marriage and family by default and it reflected in their parenting and overall happiness. How fortunate we are to now live in a time where we can make decisions based on what suits us best and what truly fills our soul.

I have no regrets about making this decision as it has granted me freedom unknown to most. Solitude, sleeping in, travel, an impeccably clean house, and copious amounts of wine are just some of the perks of being childfree. In my conversations with others, I have been completely transparent about my choice to be childfree, and I have met some incredible men and women that share my views. Instantly this bond of understanding and inclusivity is born. As I started writing and speaking to many people, I realized this book needs to be published sooner rather than later. It was evident that we needed to have more conversations around this topic and my book needed to fall into the hands of someone who really needed it.

Chapter 2
Society's Views on Your Decision

The most overwhelming part of deciding to follow your purpose rather than the path that was set for you is the backlash from society and the ones who love you most. When we step outside of traditional cultural expectations, it is very difficult for others to understand our choices. Not being understood or supported is something I believe can change once we tell our story and accept the differences amongst all of us.

A timeline has been created on how our life should pan out, so when someone ventures off of the structured path, society has taught us to believe we won't have a promising future. Many stigmas are attached to the woman who chooses not to get married and have children - they are selfish, shallow, infertile, and considered unwanted goods. We are following traditions from two centuries ago where procreation was encouraged to offset the losses the population was facing, none of which are an issue in our current day. This disconnect begins with a generational shift and how women now want to follow their dreams and aspirations. Going against the expectations was simply not a favorable option for older generations. Having children was a practical matter that generated the survival of government policies and religious organizations, which included economic benefits for businesses.

The patriarchal system is engrained at birth. We are given mini-kitchens and baby dolls as our first toys, subconsciously preparing us for our domestic duties. In schools, parenthood was assumed, and any alternative lifestyle was merely unacknowledged or treated as troublesome. As we grow older we are asked *when* we are having children, not *if*. Social persuasion can be one of the greatest struggles in coming to terms with your decision and can result in unwanted children just to be dissolved of this pressure. We all want a purpose in life and since womanhood has historically been interchangeable with motherhood, then surely you will find the fulfillment you have been looking for all along once you have a child. This is the false narrative we are all encouraged to believe.

There are stereotypes and shame attached to being childless - you are not a true woman. The term alone represents a loss of something. Just because one may be biologically capable, does not mean they have the biological instinct. Unfortunately, there is a huge misrepresentation of those who do not have kids. They are barricaded into a singular group because it's the biological destiny for all women to bear children. As the demographic of childless women grows, it's become harder to contain them within these stereotypes because they often are a diverse group with different reasonings for choosing this lifestyle. In fact, there are three major subsections to this group: childfree, childless, and by circumstance.

Women are not the only ones susceptible to this pronatalism mindset - men are experiencing it every day as well. For a man, having children shows he is full of vitality, gives the family surname a chance to live on, and provides the opportunity to leave behind some sort of legacy. When speaking to Don (a 35-year-old school teacher) about if he knew he always wanted to have children his response was, "My family indirectly played a role in this because I felt for some odd reason a responsibility to give my parents a grandchild/great-grandchild." Just as women get asked about marriage and parenthood, men are finding themselves having to answer the same questions.

Age has never been a friend of the female - marriage should be entered by a certain age, you need to have children by 30 to maximize your fertility, and as you get older your body and skin changes, reminding you that your value is decreasing. When talking to two of my male contributors I asked if their lack of a biological clock provided them more comfort surrounding having children, since they have the luxury of changing their mind at any time. One stated, "Absolutely. I would say it certainly allows us more flexibility and, in a way, dilutes the sense of urgency to procreate. Alternatively, if we were to be governed by a constantly depleting biological clock, then we would be far more compelled to make a decision earlier on." The other man said, "My biological clock is technically the same as my wife's. We knew we wanted children so we both were on her timeline."

I've learned to disregard the negative commentary and labels placed upon me simply because they are untrue. When told that my decision is selfish, I disagree wholeheartedly. I find those who have children to fulfill a missing part in themselves or their marriage without pondering the environmental impact or emotional and financial strain to be selfish. I also find it extremely self-serving that there is an expectation that your children will take care of you in your old age. Instead of telling me "I will change my mind" or "It's different when they are your own," I challenge others to consider the positive aspects of this radical act I have decided to embark on. Life has always entailed a plethora of choices and we must begin to understand that a legacy can be left behind without bearing children.

Chapter 3
The Evolution of Suzy Homemaker

For centuries we have had a system of gender roles, yet like the evolutionary species we are, things are bound to change, progress, and develop. Many cultures still adhere to the patriarchal society introduced so long ago, which is clashing with the ever-growing popularity of women forging different paths than generations before them. When Betty Friedan published *The Feminine Mystique* in 1963, there was a gentle sigh of relief from women all over when they realized that they were not alone in feeling dissatisfied with their role as the suburban housewife; after all, it was supposed to be the ultimate dream and path to feminine fulfillment.

13

In 1966, the National Organization for Women was founded to promote the equality of women in our society and dedicated themselves to creating change through lobbying, rallies, and conferences. Women were already given the right to vote but demanded more than just enfranchisement. This is where the second wave of feminism started, and women began to deviate from the domestic female paradigm. Women were now allowed to honor the thought that they might want more out of life than just their husbands and children. 100 years after being given the right to vote, it is still the first and only right that the constitution specifically affirms equality for women and men. Therefore, The Equal Rights Amendment (ERA) is a proposed amendment that *"equality of rights under the law shall not be abridged by the United States or by any state on the account of sex"* yet, 12 states still have not ratified this as of today.

With the popularity of educated women applying for the same jobs as their male counterparts, the concept that you must get married and have children is becoming less likely than it was back in the 1950s. Women today and their view on this subject matter has also vastly changed. Families in the 60s and 70s maintained secrecy when it came to family matters and their goal was to depict the perfect American family. Today, we openly accept our failures, seek therapy, and discuss topics without a filter. When Stacey (a 46-year-old childfree relationship coach) shared her interview responses with her mother for feedback, her mom was taken back by her willingness to share her story so openly, which is not an unusual thought for our mothers from that era. Stacey added, "It seems our generation is way more authentic and have realized that by sharing and being vulnerable we can connect more."

In the December 1986 issue of Ms. Magazine, respected journalist Lindsy Van Gelder wrote an article called *Countdown to Motherhood: When Should You Have a Baby?* I was inspired to read about the vast growth we have achieved since the mid-80s and equally disheartened by the struggles that working mothers faced decades prior, many of which are still prevalent today. In her article, Van Gelder recounts her first pregnancy at the age of 25. For her mother's generation, this was considered a borderline geriatric pregnancy while many of her friends were taking themselves seriously in the workplace and, "most of them were high on their newfound discovery that it was possible to break out of the engagement/marriage/quit work/baby lockstep."

Since the publication of this article 34 years ago, it's difficult to believe that our national maternity leave is still as antiquated as the notion that "a woman's place is in the kitchen." The U.S. federal Family and Medical Leave Act (FMLA) only offers 12 weeks of unpaid parental leave and only about 60% of workers are eligible. Working, for the sole purpose of paying for childcare doesn't seem optimal for the parent or the child. As most Americans can identify with, half of Van Gelder's pay went straight to a babysitter. We also need to recognize as a society that it is becoming nearly impossible to survive in a one-income household. This statistic can heavily influence the millennial woman's choice to have children. If being a working mom is necessary to maintain financial security, these ladies are pondering if they want to be utterly exhausted and have just one back-breaking job or two. In addition, they have to ask themselves if they want to be a powerful female in the workplace or win the mother of the year award. With the demands of both titles, it truly comes down to being great at one thing or average at both. If we can get over the shame placed on males and redefine masculinity perhaps it makes more sense for the female to be the bread-winner while the father is the primary caregiver.

Van Gelder highlights that having babies in one's 40s or only having one child is "less like an option and more like a necessity - the only way professional women can hope to call some of the shots." It is a statement that still holds legitimacy and accuracy. As our roles and responsibilities change and the expected contributions from each partner increases the family dynamic shifts. This no longer constricts women to their excessively domestic role as Suzy Homemaker and in turn, most men are aiding in household chores.

Chapter 4
How Your Past May Dictate Your Future

My mother was the epitome of who you would imagine leading the PTA meetings. She kept a well-run household with a stocked fridge and washing machine on a constant spin cycle, yet it seemed her idea of motherhood was rules and routine. Due to her upbringing, freely expressing emotions was somewhat of a foreign concept. She would stuff them into the deepest part of her being, but they would often bubble up to the surface leaving me feeling like I was a burden or regret.

I have now been assured that none of that is true, however, I can't help but wonder if she ever regretted her choices. Did she want more out of life? Or did she not even know better because she was so influenced by the times she had lived in? I can't blame her for not stepping out of what society expected of her, I'm 34 years younger and still having to explain myself.

I often see a cycle of mother-daughter begrudge that results in the disinterest of procreating. For me, it goes beyond that, but my mom's demeanor at times definitely played a role in me not wanting to repeat the pattern. Quite frankly, none of the females in my family seemed enamored by their role, it was just their fate. They never abandoned their children or were negligent, but it surely didn't appear like parenting was always a blessing. It seemed burdensome, tiring, and an experience where you often felt as if you lost yourself as an individual. For someone who was on the fence, the female role models in my life did not sell the idea. I can get an honest moment out of my closest girlfriends who mutter, "Don't have kids!" Of course, they love their children and their brutal honesty usually comes during the midst of a mommy meltdown, but it still holds some weight. Having children is a life-altering decision and it needs to be seriously considered.

Parenting is hard regardless of whether you wanted to have children or not. We as women are scorned by society if we are vocal about wanting to remain childless or speak of the frustration or regrets over the choices we have made. It is taboo to admit that our expectations of having children fail us at times and it's not always an abundance of happiness, joy, and love. Amy Schumer expresses in her HBO documentary *Expecting Amy,* "I don't resent being pregnant. I resent everyone who hasn't been honest. I resent the culture and how much women have to suck it the fuck up and act like everything is fine. I really resent that." Women in particular have been conditioned to romanticize the feeling children have brought them. Certainly, there are moments you share with your child that undoubtedly are blissful and worth the challenges, but that doesn't mean that your only source of happiness comes from being a parent. Brandon (37-year-old Marine Veteran) discussed the struggles attached to parenting and exclaims, "It can, and will, fucking suck! Ever notice that whenever you ask parents about how things are going, they always tend to say, 'things are great' or 'couldn't be happier'. That's all a front to try to avoid sounding like an unloving parent or labeling their child as a psychopath that runs the household. No one will ever freely denounce their child, but the fact of the matter is that it can and will be stressful and energy draining." All parents will admit that having a child is life-altering, but only a very few will express the hardships, challenges, and lack of personal choices that come along with their decision. Stacey recalls when her family was uprooted from the States and moved to London for a job opportunity her father took two weeks after Stacey's mom gave birth to her younger sister. "[Her] hormones were going crazy from postpartum. Dealing with moving to a new country is a huge stressor especially when you're breastfeeding but she took it like a champ. This was also the first time I saw my mom cry. With all the travel I guess my sister came down with ITP and I know my mom must have been so scared. My dad was in finance and that was the reason we moved so [he] was completely focused on this new job and it must have been very lonely for my mom to deal with this all on her own." Like many mothers, Stacey's mom put her personal needs aside and championed for the family without murmuring that she needed help. Stacey continued by saying, "A lot of moms go through this but feel shame in admitting it. I think moms are getting more open about this and just hope it keeps going that way, so they feel supported."

I have also witnessed men and women who have taken their less-than-desirable upbringing and used it as a driving force to love their child unconditionally and place them before anything else. One of the women I interviewed shared about her troubled past with her own mom and said, "She was around until I was about six then she was gone because she decided it wasn't for her…but I never thought I would be like her because I love children. I knew I could do it. I knew what I *did not* want to be like." Brandon had a similar experience and recalls, "Fatherhood to me was to not become my own father: two marriages, three children, and working 16-hour days. I still respected my father and he tried his best given the circumstances, but I did believe it was an example of what not to do." This upbringing set standards for Brandon and ultimately is what saved his marriage when he was in the midst of dark days caused by irrevocable decisions. He had found comfort in another woman when he was at a boiling point with a strenuous workload, an infant suffering from colic, and an unappreciative wife. Brandon expressed, "I betrayed my wife and thus gave a path for my daughter to live a similar childhood to my own, separate households, two Christmases, and a tension-filled custody exchange each week. I needed to repair the damage that I caused in my house, and I made it a determination to make things right again."

We now are exposed to this "having it all" mentality but maybe that isn't necessary to have a successful life. Whenever women are labeled selfish for not having children, I think it's important to understand the selflessness that comes with making that choice to not have children. I know what the demands are of having a child and I am also fully aware of my limitations, some of which have a direct conflict of interest. I know the kind of mother I would want to be, and I am also very honest that I don't have the competence for it. I have witnessed the damage done to children through experiences they had in their formative years and I am not willing to take that risk on. I am still trying to figure out how to love myself unconditionally and obtaining that is most important.

Growing up, I always was exposed to many older females that I admired who did not have children by choice. I was fascinated by the wonderful lives they lived. I quickly realized I didn't *have* to have children when I grew up. Instead of focusing on my gender expectations, I concentrated on my interests and curiosities as a young child that allowed me to find my destiny and decide what contributions I wanted to make to this world. Decades later, I realize that not all women were exposed to alternative lifestyles in their childhood. Marie (44-year-old self-proclaimed crazy cat lady) grew up in a small town in Texas and explained how females get married near the age of 20 and start having children. With this traditional but narrow mindset still entrenched in their town, she worries deeply about her nieces' future. She ponders about how she wants more for them and says, "Their goal in life has always been to be a mom. Which is great, but then what happens if they struggle and they can't. Then I think that was the only thing you wanted to do your entire life and you put all your identity around it and so, now what do you do?"

Natalia's (known as the posh and eclectic aunt to her 15 nieces & nephews) outlook when she realized she would never be a mom was, "I'm okay with it. I learned a different way to thrive and I'm fine with it and super happy about that choice because I do believe in a higher power and this was not really meant for me and it's okay." Hopefully, females like Marie's nieces will be able to adopt this mindset as well and create a successful future for themselves even if they initially feel their hopes and dreams have been derailed.

Chapter 5
Navigating Through Choices

There are many various reasons why people choose to have children as well as choose not to. The top factors people consider range from whether they have the means to provide their child with a good life, deciding if they want to bring a human into this scary and uncertain world, to whether they would like to live out their existence on their own terms. All of these are valid and may hold different rankings for each individual. For those that have no maternal/paternal instinct, it helps alleviate uncertainty but does not eliminate the hesitation about moving forward confidently in a pronatalism society. As I said previously, I knew from a very young age that the desire to grow up and start a family was not particularly a goal for me. The traits and temperament it takes to be a good mother were not ones I had in my vault. I truly feel like I can leave a better footprint on my community and this world by remaining childless because the undertaking of raising children would undoubtedly pull me away from the things I cherish and am passionate about. I value my freedom and independence; it's what makes my life so fulfilling and I wouldn't want to resent my child for taking that away from me.

The discussions I had with the males that have children were riveting. They conveyed in descriptive detail about their experiences with fatherhood. In a candid conversation, I had one man tell me that he never wanted children and regrets the choice he made to have them. He continued discussing with me how he does love his children, but if he could do it over, he would have done things differently. Some may find this to be a horrendous statement, but I valued his honesty and ability to admit this with little apprehension. I'm sure it's not an easy feeling to come to terms with. On the contrary, Nick (a 43-year-old father of two girls) exclaimed, "It is really amazing watching these little humans change and grow and brings back a lot of memories from growing up. It allows you to revisit your own childhood and share the experience with your own children."

During a podcast interview, Matthew McConaughey shared that, "Some of my most comfortable roles has been playing a father or father figure and I think that's because the one thing I knew I wanted to be in life was a father. I knew that since I was eight years old." I have seen babies brought into this world that have filled a void and given individuals a reason to live. My brother happens to be one of those people. I honestly can't say for certain that he would be alive if it hadn't been for the birth of his daughter.

Even though Nick always wanted children and a major part of getting married was to raise a family, he didn't minimize the struggles that come with it. "We have been very fortunate. Our children are both physically and mentally healthy. [My wife] and I have rewarding careers and solid meaningful relationships with friends and family. With all of those factors working in our favor, it is still a ton of work. I don't think non-parents realize how much work it is. Your sleep is impacted and that can trickle down into every aspect of your life. It makes working harder, it makes being patient with your spouse harder and it makes being good to yourself harder. I can't imagine how hard it is for parents with special needs children or single parents. It is so much work!"

Many other people are daunted by the financial costs it takes to raise a child. Multiple sources calculate the cost of raising one child from birth until age 18 to be just under $250,000. These are necessary costs like food, shelter, health care, and education. This number does not include unforeseeable circumstances or extracurricular expenses. One of my male contributors, Don, who has a six-month-old said, "Conservatively, where we live you will need a minimum of $800 a month for food, diapers, baby stuff, etc. which is a constant as they grow. That's saying you have someone to watch them as well." It also is noteworthy that this is just until 18 - most parents intend on covering the cost of college, weddings and supporting those that end up boomeranging back to their parents' house after previously living on their own. Vikas (a single 35-year-old real estate agent) said, "So there are the obvious talking points; finances, the ability to provide shelter and food, and most importantly the time, energy, and affection that you must allocate to the child, all while maintaining the sanctity of your marriage. These are the basics points you must address, but the one that I urge future parents to consider is how committed to the cause they are because raising a child is the easy part but raising a good child, now that's the winning ticket."

Brandon has been straightforward with the not so glamorous parts of parenthood but also states, "My favorite aspect of being a father rests in the idea that I helped raise this little human into a growing, functional, sarcastic little shit that I adore beyond compare. My daughter, as with all humans, has her flaws and will drive me up the walls, but at this moment, she is the most perfect person that I know."

Another concern that emerges is the state of our world, from safety to the environment. My fondest childhood memories were riding my bicycle around my neighborhood and not returning until the porch light came on - my mom's signal that dinner was ready.

Now, allowing children to play unsupervised is risky and worrisome. We know the impact our choices have had on our environment and as the decades go on, it's an apparent downward spiral. Not only does reproduction contribute to the negative impact of excess carbon emissions, but one must ask themselves if they are comfortable with leaving their offspring to survive in an inhospitable world. Without having a conversation with yourself and your partner about all the inter-workings of parenthood, things could become perilous. Vikas added, "I feel a prerequisite to parenthood should include looking at it from a practical perspective and not simply a primal instinct to procreate. This is so important because it compels us to evaluate the reasons for our decisions and the environment in which the child will grow up in."

Women have worked hard over the past years to break glass ceilings and they are thriving! With the success of having careers, reaching ambitious goals, and creating remarkable experiences it's hard to decide if they are ready to make the sacrifice to have all that come to a screeching halt and focus on getting pregnant. Even though you are assured you'll be able to handle it all, something naturally requires you to be less involved. One thing that can weigh heavy on your mind is questioning if you will have any regrets about your choice later in life. When I asked Stacey, who has remained childfree, her response was "Absolutely zero. No question. Not once." Although when Vikas was asked the same question, he stated "That's a difficult question. I think the last day of life will reveal all the right and wrong decisions we've made with our time on planet Earth. I can only speak for this moment right now, the present with the information I have at hand, and it tells me that it would not be responsible to pursue a family unit at this time."

As for me, I know there are moments I will never experience since I am not a mom, but never have I felt those would outweigh having to give up all the other things I have because I am not a mother.

Chapter 6
Dealing With Circumstances

"When are you having kids?" can be a very exasperating question for the woman who made her choice, but it can be utterly heartrending for others who had a great desire to become a mother but were faced with the unsettling realization that they would never become pregnant and alternative choices to raising a child were not available to them. There is this flawed idea that because you were born with ovaries and a uterus that reproduction is a sure bet. "Infertility is a weird thing to discuss with people who have not gone through it. I would notice friends would clam up, or just get quiet when I would bring it up. After time, I decided to speak only to friends who could relate on some level," stated Christine. Infertility simply put is when you and your partner are unable to achieve getting pregnant after having frequent unprotected sex, but there can be many other contributing factors. Endometriosis, for instance, causes the lining to grow outside the uterus. You can still conceive, but the chances are much more difficult. Polycystic Ovary Syndrome often referred to as PCOS, is a hormonal disorder in which a woman's ovaries fail to regularly release eggs. In addition to those who can't get pregnant, there are the women who do but experience the devastating loss of reoccurring miscarriages. Now, let's revisit the initial question, "When are you having kids?" It may be innocent, but it also can be absolutely soul-crushing for some.

One of my male contributors, Brandon, opened up about the effect that his wife's miscarriage had on him. His wife went to her end of the first-trimester checkup and so far, things were progressing fine with her pregnancy. When she returned home, she threw herself into his arms, sobbing and distraught. He said, "I knew that this could be her reaction to one event, we lost our child. I joined her in the sorrow but mine did not last long as I needed to comfort my wife. After several hours, my wife was eventually calmed, and I packed my duffel bag to head into work. During my hour-long drive into my station, I did my normal routine: listened to my podcasts, sipped on my pre-workout, and knocked out a complete workout in the station gym prior to my shift start." Brandon continues to explain how he went through his customary regimen and then exclaimed, "I closed my locker then it hit me like a freight train, I lost my child. I collapsed onto my bench in an uncontrolled sob and punched my locker and myself in order to snap myself out of it before my coworkers heard me, but one of my coworkers did hear me and walked over to me...I told this man what had happened, and his response was simple, 'Go home and be with your wife, we will be alright,' referring to my coworkers. I returned home to a shocked but grateful wife, as she was not expecting me to return for another 12 hours. I remained home for a week as we struggled to heal, however, together." Two years later, "I finally achieved the goal of becoming a father, and after we had battled through the pain of a miscarriage, it finally seemed that my wife and I had cleared the most massive pregnancy hurdle that was ever thrown our way," Brandon recalled.

We are all aware of the looming biological clock, which seems to be a mere folklore until you reach your early 30s. Unfortunately, not everyone finds themselves in a serious relationship by this age, resulting in giving up on their dream of motherhood or seeking alternative options. For those who want to continue on the path of becoming a mother, they normally are left with IVF, which can be painful, costly, and consists of multiple rounds to ensure success. For those who decide to adopt, the process can be lengthy and emotionally overwhelming. I was privileged enough to speak with multiple women, all of which had intentions of having biological children, but uncontrollable issues emerged and impacted their decision. Even though their experiences and outcomes were vastly different, they shared a common outcome of still living a fulfilled life.

One of my contributors was Christine, a very career-driven woman who knew that she wanted to be a mom one day but her main focus at that moment was accomplishing her other goals first. At 32 she met her husband and a year later they actively started trying to conceive. Christine recalls, "After three years of being unsuccessful though, we decided to see a [fertility] specialist…we sought this help because we were realistic; we were getting older and had no luck." While on vacation her doctor phoned with her blood test results, which were not favorable. Christine stated, "I will never forget this day, this moment, and that feeling I had. I literally felt hopeless. I didn't even know what the results she shared really meant. I had no time to research but I knew it was bad, and it was going to be a long journey ahead, with no guarantee of success and also expensive." Even with the chips stacked against them, Christine and her husband continued on their path to parenthood. "A miracle happened. We were actually in an IVF cycle, our fifth attempt at trying to conceive. We were waiting to hear if I was pregnant and during that time, we got a life-changing call. An estranged family member had a child, however, was not in a position to raise a child. Without a second thought, my husband

and I actively worked to adopt this beautiful baby boy, which we officially did, two years after he was born," explained Christine.

Some women were truly born to be mothers and will go to great lengths to fulfill their desire to have a family. On the contrary, some decide that the uncontrollable variables they have been presented with led them to find their life's purpose in some other way. One of my sources became pregnant once in her early teens and again in her late twenties. She made the tough decision to terminate both pregnancies because of uncontrollable circumstances. When she approached 42, she found herself desperately wanting a child. After spending thousands of dollars and overcoming the failure associated with not being able to get pregnant she got to a point where she accepted it wasn't meant to be. Her past pregnancies never came at the right time and although this has ultimately left her childless, she would still make the same choices over.

Marie, who always wanted children, six to be exact, faced her own set of struggles when it came to becoming a mother. As she got older, the financial aspect of kids set in and she realized that two children were probably more suitable because she wanted to provide them with the best life she could afford. Then at 22, she was diagnosed with PCOS. She remembers her initial thought being, "Shit. That's going to make it harder and I don't want to deal with that. Then I never found the right partner so I thought I would do it alone…because I would be okay with doing that, but then it just kept getting further and further away and when I hit age 35 I thought I don't want to start with a baby at 35! I'll be in my 50s when they're a teenager! So, it just kind of rolled into where I am now and I'm good with it."

As a female who endured both physical and emotional pain due to the spontaneous loss of her baby, Natalia's advice to women who can't get pregnant is, "Instead of putting all your hopes and dreams into a child who's going to carry on your legacy, you just do it yourself. It's not the end-all and you either have a choice to just move forward and get joy somewhere else because you certainly are going to wallow away, never grow, and it won't serve you well to linger on it at all. I look back and I'm like you know what? I'm glad because I have a lot of opportunities that some of my friends can't have or don't have because they have children and that's great."

Men deal with their own set of circumstances. Don explained, "I had set many target dates for myself to make things happen or for things to happen naturally. Personally, I would have stayed single and probably childless if I hadn't met the right person by 35. After that, I knew that I would be unwilling to give up my lifestyle to raise a child into my early 70s."

However, Vikas expressed, "If both my partner and I were very passionate about having children and we didn't have the natural means to do it then I would say all options are on the table. There's no reason to abstain from one choice over the other. My first choice would probably be adoption. I think there are plenty of children out there who need love and affection and don't have it."

Parenthood is more than just passing on genetics and DNA. It is about being responsible for the well-being of another human mentally, physically, and emotionally. Christine added, "The more I think about it, the more I come to grips with the fact that while I always meant to be a mom, and my husband a dad, perhaps we were also meant to save a little life." A statement that was utterly profound and heartwarming to hear.

Including the struggles of conceiving was paramount to incorporate in this book. All too often we assume the back story of each individual and as the stories in this chapter illuminate, there is a wide spectrum on what many undergo, and how compassion and empathy are essential. Christine further explained, "Because of our unique circumstances, people felt they had every right to ask really personal things. This always shocked me because, with the questions that were being asked, you could tell that judgment was being passed. With some questions, I often found myself justifying everything, or feeling the need to." The path to parenthood is different for everyone and the struggles do not end once the baby is born. The development of your child and who they become as young adults and beyond can be difficult as well. We all wish for smart, healthy, and thriving children but unexpected challenges in learning development, mental illness, physical ailments, and addiction could arise. These are never situations we want to entertain as possibilities, but your capability and commitment should be considered if you are going to embark on becoming a parent who may endure these unfortunate circumstances since parenthood is truly a lifetime commitment. It's also worth noting that there will be an equally arduous emotional side: it will ache when they can't use words to tell you where it hurts, witnessing them getting picked on or bullied, and of course their first heartbreak. With all that said, one of my sources stated, "It gives you a chance to relive life again through the eyes of your child. Both small and big moments. It's amazing to see the joy they get out of simple things that we as adults often forget because for them they are discovering it for the first time."

Chapter 7
Just the Two of Us

A couple's journey to making their decision on parenthood is extremely important. There are a few alternative types of childless couples: some who have decided early on to have a future without children, those who postponed the decision which ultimately led them to a childless lifestyle or an "acquisitor" who adapts to the idea of a childfree life because of their spouse. It has always been mind-blowing speaking to couples that have never encroached on the topic of their personal desires about children. For me personally, that is a question I would dive right into on the first date! Since my preference is steadfast, it would be a waste of time to further a courtship with someone who wanted to start a brood of children. Brandon declared, "I knew without a doubt that I did want children at an early age. During my dating years, many of my relationships with women lasted a minimum of a year and I searched the region for a woman to become my wife and eventually mother to my children." Brandon continued to say, "People need to understand that starting a family is not easy, nor should it be…but more importantly, I want to highlight the power a love for one's child has on the mind."

A problem in our society is the lack of thought when considering parenthood and in hindsight realizing they should have waited or not become parents at all. If significant discussions around the struggles of parenthood are vague or nonexistent, new parents can be overwhelmed by their new reality. Don shared the struggles he and his wife faced and said, "The first is not being on the same page with parental decisions. From names to circumcision, it all gets laid out on the table and unless you are both of like-mind someone will always feel like they have lost.

Another thing is, your relationship starts to take a hit. You no longer can go on a date night whenever you want and forget getting your rocks off when you want to. Family will also have their own ideas which you will either begrudgingly let them do to make them happy or you will hold fast, set boundaries, and piss them off. It seems everyone thinks they are entitled to your kid in some way or form."

If you and your partner can honestly say that you are willing to have your life altered, you've accomplished your goals, and have experienced many of the things you've always wanted, while understanding that parenting can be difficult and unpredictable, then you probably are ready for parenthood. Nick feels people really need to ask themselves the tough questions before making the decision to start a family. He said, "If you feel it deep down in your soul, you should have kids. If you aren't sure or are asking yourself questions about it, I would wait. My brother and his wife are not going to have children and they have always been on the same page about it. They are very happy." Brandon has devoted his life to service - Marine Corps, police officer, and now raising a child that he hopes becomes more successful than him. He's always felt there is a bigger world than just himself and states, "I could have been all about myself - never served, make good money in a safe industry, date numerous women on short term basis, travel on a whim, but at the end of my time what could I really hang my hat on? I have friends that fit in this category and I honestly feel bad for them, they are getting into their older years and when they go home it is an empty house."

When couples decide together that they want to be a childless couple, it helps not only how they forge out their future plans but it also creates a unified bond when answering questions to family and friends. I, myself, am in one of these partnerships and it is a very secure feeling knowing I have someone by my side with unwavering support. When interviewing Vikas for a male perspective he said, "I would have to say that earlier on I fully embraced the idea of having children. I saw myself in a family unit, however as I grew older, I started to realize that logic dictates that I first take care of myself and those that I love before I take on the immense responsibility of trying to manage a family. This perspective can be viewed as selfish but I see it as exactly the opposite. To me, it is about giving the decision its due respect."

Often, a couple may marry with the thought of children one day but before they know it, years have passed, they are at the pinnacle of their career, and still have a list of places they want to explore. Ultimately, they realize that children are likely not going to happen even though at one point they believed starting a family was something they wanted. Natalia, who had been married to her husband for over 10 years and was 36 years old at the time, suffered from a miscarriage well into her 2nd trimester. She specifically explained the impact it had on her spouse, "I think it's made us stronger and he hasn't let it define him. It's sad when he thinks about it, but he's also very independent and learned that wasn't in the cards and you go on and make another life for yourself."

Lastly, those who identify as an acquisitor did see kids in their future, but the time spent with their partner made them realize their relationship is more important than being in a partnership with another person who would provide them with that family unit they once dreamt of.

I know that a fulfilling life can be achieved with just my partner and me. As much as we don't mind being around kids, we are so thankful that at the end of the day the life we have built is determined by choices we make with our best interests in mind. We make choices individually and together that help us attain mutual happiness. To me, that holds a higher value than raising a child.

Chapter 8
Your Journey Begins Now

As I mentioned in the introduction, this book isn't meant to steer you clear of parenthood or lead you to the same choices I have, but rather to help you make sure you truly have pondered the realities that come with having a child. I've been told a million times over "I might change my mind," and although I respectfully disagree, you may still be unsure. Luckily, there are options to allow women in this day and age to seek out lifestyles without having to fully give up on the dream of one day becoming a mother. From adoption to freezing your eggs, there are a plethora of alternatives instead of making a rash decision because of the ever-looming biological clock. First and foremost, if you are not currently ready to start a family then some form of birth control should be non-negotiable. All too often women are finding themselves standing with a positive pregnancy test and filled with gloom and hopelessness. This is not just the female in her early 20s that made some irresponsible decisions, these are mothers that are not able to handle bringing another child into this world. I am a major advocate for reproductive rights but do not support using abortion as a repetitive form of birth control. A close source recalled her multiple abortions and made the decision to terminate her pregnancy because she knew "there was no way I could do that, at least not do it right." Even though her circumstances at the time did not allow for a child, 47 years later after her first abortion she adds, "You don't forget them… I'll tell you that much."

My hopes are that reading this book has brought you some kind of comfort in your decision about whether or not to have children, or at least a better appreciation for those who have a varying opinion from you. Don added that, "I would say minus your job, are you willing to give up all the things you like doing at this moment? If the answer is no, you're not ready. This isn't to say that you don't get to do them, it's just a matter of could you walk away if you had to. I still do things, I see friends, I work out, I do things I enjoy, but there are many things I have come to the conclusion that I cannot do anymore or at the moment and I am okay with it." Another contributor Nick stated, "I knew 100% that I wanted kids. But even with that, I needed to have the right partner and be in a good place career-wise." After years of facing this controversial conversation, I realized that we need to open up the dialogue about why we are living childless. Hopefully, this starts spreading awareness for those who forego parenthood and deconstruct the associated stigmas. The empowerment of women in our society is increasing and the paradigm of gender roles and expectations must shift as well.

Resources

Expecting Amy. Directed by Alexander Hammer, performances by Amy Schumer, HBOMax, 2020.

Friedan, Betty. The Feminine Mystique. New York: Norton, 2013.

Rogan, Joe, host. "#1552- Matthew McConaughey." The Joe Rogan Experience 22 Oct. 2020 open.spotify.com/episode/15eJWDILCbXFI3B2whkBTr?si= hfgxfc10SQyBTsURPNHCyQ

Van Gelder, Lindsy. "Countdown To Motherhood: When Should You Have A Baby". Ms. Magazine, Vol. XV, No. 6, Dec. 1986, p. 38

Acknowledgments

To my contributors- Brandon, Carla, Christine, Don, Jes, Marie, Natalia, Nick, Stacey, and Vikas- you brought this book alive by sharing your struggles and introspection to give the reader the support they needed.

Mom- If it wasn't for you making the ultimate sacrifice to put your needs aside to raise my brothers and me, I would have never had the opportunity to put this book into the hands of those that need it most.

Kaveesh- My partner I'm doing this thing called life with. Thank you for your unwavering support, encouragement to leap before I know how to fly, speak my mind without apprehension, and put ink to paper without a care in the world as to who I might offend because doing anything other than that would be hiding the quirky, resilient, and passionate soul that I am.

EP- For helping me with this book baby from when it was just a thought to when it became an actual paperback.

Kim & Sara- Thank you for blessing me with those earthbound angels and allowing me to be your child's godmother, something that is such a precious title to me and you can find solace that I will always champion for those children without hesitation.

Gigi & Trupps- Since you entrusted me with revealing the gender of your baby, I thought what better way to introduce your baby GIRL into the world!

All the females in my life who have inspired me and taught me that glass ceilings are meant to be shattered.

And lastly, to myself- Learning to say "no" without guilt, and "yes" without fear.

About the Author

Ashton Saldana is a writer and the founder of Soulace Seeker, a blog focused on relationships, travel, spirituality, and women empowerment. After filing for divorce partly due to the conflicting views on parenthood with her then spouse, she faced the aftermath of a failed marriage and the shame placed upon her by society. In all of this, she gained confidence in her choice and became a confidant to other women struggling with their own internal battles regarding whether or not becoming a mother was for them. She self-published her first book, *Words From the Soul* in October 2018 which is currently available on Amazon and in local indie bookstores.

Made in the USA
Monee, IL
20 February 2021

60137102R00046